D1552730

Chapter One – 1934

The young lady shook her head,

Seeing her reflection in the river's bed.

Blond hair and eyes of brown,

Her heart, her soul, one of definite down.

Getting to her delicate feet,

The heart gave a startled leap.

A man standing with a smile on his face,

His body one of a smelly disgrace.

He grabbed her by the arms so tight,

Her heart gave a jumping fright.

Then he threw her to the ground that night,

Taking from her, what wasn't his right.

She awoke hours later, scared and cold,

Her body numb, no feeling of bold.

So gathering her clothes, she ran towards home,

For some warmth, and an uncaring dome.

Her mother then gave her daughter a toss,

"How could you give us such a loss?

You are nothing, but useless slime,

Don't come to me and waste my time!"

Now you must marry, of course,

Don't you dare show me some remorse.

Do go now, right away!

Don't even think you won't do what I say!"

So she married within a year,

Many a night she shed many a tear.

Her husband then was hardly there,

Young lady just combed her long hair.

Then the children began to be born,

One after another, never alone.

But not knowing how to show true love,

Abuse formed like clouds above.

She knew not how to raise her children,

But her *Bible* gave her a little wisdom.

The world matters kept getting in her way,

Bringing anger to her children each day.

Oh NO, the child crawled across the kitchen floor,

Dad's foot kicked her behind once more!

Brother's screams heard behind the door,

He'd been locked to quiet the poor!

Scared Baby Fay, thirstily cried in her crib,

Down her throat, the mom stuffed a bib.

To quiet the child for a short time,

This so mom could have peace of mind.

Bats in the attic, also there,

Pulling on the children's hair.

Terror at night from the bat's flight,

No peace was known in day or night!

Brother then burned down the city library,

He was now feeling so contrary.

Of the abuse to his body and mind,

Child abuse, in another time!

Mother always flailed at her man,

"I married you and look at your clan!

You're nothing and I'm in command,

Listen to me, I demand!"

The husband sat in his rocking chair,

Slowly, his life took away his hair.

Dying silently with a solemn stare,

His eyes, showed pain, within the glare…..

Mom went to a nursing home,

Never, ever to be alone.

Reading books all throughout the day,

Nothing nice, ever to say.

When she died, no one cried,

Didn't care, she was no longer alive.

Chapter Two – Baby Fay

Years later, Fay met a man,

Soon, she too, had a brooding clan.

Not knowing how to love a child,

Fay, became, increasingly wild!

Her children went where they did not declare,

Off to the store, without a care.

No food, no clothes, the house a mess,

Father always gone, just like the rest.

It was whispered, she was a mother!

For the children, she had borne.

But she really was another,

Melting in the setting sun!

So many thought got in her way,

Shooting stars within her mind did play.

As she passed the day away,

She never knew any kind words to say.

Creek beds were for her laughter,

This abused lonely daughter.

Deserts were her only fun,

While she learned how she could run.

Now the trees never lose their leaves,

There is silence everywhere.

Fay, it seemed, never learned anything.

And I cry, nobody cared, it seemed.

Chapter Three – Fay's Child

As a child of four, I sat by the sea,

Watching dad, dip his net gracefully.

Bringing up the net, always full of fish,

Silver sparkles, among the moon's mist.

He dumped them into big white cans,

Their home no longer the sea, now it was mans.

He carried them off to be our main dish,

These fish were my father's greatest wish.

So heading to home, my siblings and I,

Dad gave a sad, discontented sigh.

Little Julie began to cry,

But nobody even asked her why.

I cry because I am hungry,

Oh to have some food.

I cry because I'm cold,

Oh to have some wood.

I gather a tattered blanket,

To give me some comfort.

Then huddle in a corner, where there's no one to warn her, and think,

This is life!

I guess we only know,

What our life does show.

Julie always cried and cried,

Brother Dean disappeared, and maybe died.

Chapter Four – Julie

Sister Julie was the pretty one,

Skin of silk, always full of fun.

Brown straight hair and eyes that sparkle,

Never had hand full of carpal.

A woman, one always looked up to,

Four wonderful children, within her brew.

The youngest girl, she called Loo,

All who saw her, was an angel they knew.

But at the young, tender age of two,

Doctors thought she had the Asian flu.

Later we knew it was cancer of the brain,

Sunny days became as rain.

Julie held Loo in her arms so tight,

But the Lord, claimed Loo one night.

No more soft coos from baby Loo,

She joined the angels, one day anew.

Jule sat numb within a cold, cold world,

Crying, very long, for soft baby girl.

Now asleep within our Lord Jesus,

A very hard time for all of us.

Soon Julie found an inner power.

Becoming stronger within the hour.

To this days she's one fine woman,

Always kind to every person.

For she speaks how sorrow made her strong.

This, for in life, so we can all get along!

Chapter Five – Brother Dean Disappears

Brother Dean, liked to be high,

Problems in his past show us why.

He married and had children of three,

His spirit was always flying free.

We still loved him, tried and true,

Although his mood was often blue.

He took his family to Port Angeles,

There he became under stress and duress.

His wife passed away September that year,

For his life he began to fear.

Then November, he too, disappeared,

Never since, from him have we heard.

One night, in my ear, he did say,

"Don't worry sis, I am in a fine way."

His voice sounded strong, no longer stoned,

I now knew, he'd found his home.

I still watch for him every day,

I call the police to hear what they say.

"Presumed dead, at this time,"

I learned to abide just fine.

Chapter Six – Back to 1967

I met a man, our love went calmly,

Like a clear blue sky.

Then some dark clouds came,

And you said goodbye.

Now the world is stormy,

The flowers have all died.

I miss you so much darling,

Since the day you said goodbye.

The birds that sang are forgotten,

They seem to have gone away.

And you left with them honey,

How I wish you had of stayed.

My heart is like the ocean,

As it pounds upon the shore.

Especially when I hear your name,

Then I want you all the more.

I know I will survive,

As survive, we all must,

But right now I feel as though,

My body will surely rust.

The years have gone by now in three,

I find I am marrying thee.

From now on we'll be happy and free,

I promise no big spending spree.

Together our spirits will flee,

I'll report everything to thee.

In less than a year a child we hold,

To raise correct, but not too bold.

To protect awhile from the cold,

Until this child grows so old.

But when I came from that hospital bed,

Another woman was lying there instead.

Making me wish that I was dead,

She was lying beside my husband's head.

But I never died, I only cried, took our daughter so we could all survive.

He moved to Texas, or some such state,

I divorced him on the fastest date.

Then taught our daughter to never hate,

And new ideas to contemplate.

I dated another man for four years or so,

He said my heart he'd never let go.

Treated me with dignity,

Made my spirit feel so free.

Then it happened once again,

He began a type of sin.

I was alone with my bottle of gin,

Like before, when I did begin!

Chapter Seven – The Next Eleven Years

The next eleven years,

I learned of tears!

They boxed my ears,

And shifted my gear.

Lifted my leers and enhanced my fears!

That's when I began to wonder,

If all men came on like thunder!

Then rode off into the wild blue younder!

For you see, I had remarried happily,

A handsome man, gracefully.

Times were good, and times were bad,

But not always so very sad.

But when he jumped on me with a knife to my head,

And said "You mind, or find, you will be dead!"

Well, my love at that moment it fled,

Making me with to be alone instead.

Many years to hospital with fears,

Beaten up, emotional bruises, and too many tears.

He always seemed to go out of town,

If questioned he made me feel like a clown.

Later I learned what he was doing all around,

Many people on their face had a frown.

Years later, from nowhere did they give,

A man, two sons, with us did live.

Within our home for a year or so,

These men, I never did know.

The father went to jail for awhile,

I cared for two sons, with a smile.

No money for us, but they gave fresh fish,

And magic lemons to go with this main dish.

One day, my children and I were driving slow,

Looking in the rear view window, my son fell out
the window!

I screamed and stopped, but in front of our car,

Was the man and his sons, not too far!

Time seemed stopped, shocked I looked,

My son was okay, in his car seat he was hooked.

The father and his sons were now long gone,

My children and I never knew what had gone wrong!

Then he disappeared away into the hills,

Marchie returned, shaking with chills.

We packed up and went to return to home,

Never again to go on motorcycle run.

Later I heard the man in the hills,

Shot himself in the head with kills.

My mind felt in turmoil, oh so sore,

Feeling that all was against me for evermore.

Chapter Eight – My Ride

Motorcycles began a new way of life,

Riding free in the wind, no type of strife.

My husband was now a mellow man,

We party and laughed, whenever we can.

We decided to go on a motorcycle run,

These rides were always, so much fun.

Friends gathered from all around,

Sharing stories and drinking all abound.

My friend Marchie told me of trouble,

A husband and wife, no longer a couple.

I pondered this for an hour or so,

Then talked to Marchie so I could know.

What could we do to help them through?

This trouble the couple did brew?

But Marchie started yelling "Now she knew.

Who had been spreading this gossipy goo… "

Marchie said she had only told me true,

She heard it back from me, she thought everyone knew.

I had spoken to no one but her,

She was confused, I did fear.

Soon all ladies were throwing rocks at me uninvited,

Saying, "Get out of here, your kinds not wanted!

Running as a coward, I went and wept,

Crying for three days, within my tent.

But we forgot about this incident,

Marchie and I went about our business.

Decided to go for to the woods for a walk,

When a whistling nosie came from behind a big rock.

Before us now, a man with a gun,

Saying "Don't move, or never again will you run!"

But Marchie freaked out and ran a fast gait,

I felt calm and absolute faith.

For I knew if I moved, I would be shot,

So I talked to him without a doubt.

He calmed down and said "You're Right!

I only wanted to cause you a fright!"

Chapter Nine – My Oldest Daughter

Oh my darling, how could I not see?

You were being beaten mischievously.

By a man with five children of his own,

Oh my God, how could I have not known?

My child, I see the pain deep in your soul,

Causing you to remain un-whole.

The pain to you was a violent blow,

To your head, your spirit, your natural flow.

You must look around, and you will see,

In this world so much beauty.

Jump from your head to reality,

Chemicals upon you cause calamity.

For is it not our life we make?

We lose love, our heart does break.

But strength comes to you like a stake,

Pounded into ground, our land we take.

If we cannot have what we desire,

Look up, grow strong, like a fire.

Then substitutions will aspire,

Different spirits can make you higher.

As you follow your path, over rock you fall,

This is how one's spirit grows tall.

For you know where that rock in the ground did lay,

No longer trouble upon you will play.

We've been through a lot I see,

That's where wisdom comes naturally.

Maturity comes when you are free,

Of man's block on ones mentality.

On day, my child, you will know,

Why troubles and bubbles your life did show.

Then happiness to you will all be aglow,

Because of the wisdom within your soul.

Now my three children also wanted to write,

So I told them that it was alright.

The following three stories to you will show,

What my children wanted the world to know.

Chapter Ten – "Barbara Star" by Oldest Daughter

The young star twinkled in the sky,

Music in harmony drifted by.

Mists gathered as they did fly,

While mother sang a lullaby.

The child in her bed did toss and turn,

Sadness in her heart did churn.

For a friend she loved had moved away,

How she wished she had of stayed!

As the music soothed her gentle soul,

Sleep came once again more whole.

She dreamed she was in the sky so light,

Like smoke from a distant candle bright.

She was standing away on a star,

Away, away, so very far.

Mists of sparkles blew around,

But there was silence, no earthly sound.

She waved her arms,

Had dancing charms.

She hummed gently,

Like the cool calm sea.

When suddenly a voice asked "Who art thee?"

The child said "I come from earth, It is sadness that brings my curse.

For my dear friend moved away today,

How I wish that she had of stayed."

"Dear child" said the voice, "Your friend will always be there,

Within your heart, so never fear.

In your heart and mind will declare,

So listen, my child, very clear.

If one has many friends around,

Love does eventually aboud.

So keep loved ones near within your heart,

For this is what true life is about.

Help one another when times are bad,

Then appreciate when times are glad.

For if all time was perfect and good,

How would you judge a different mood?

Now to keep you happy for times my dear,

Here's a locket for you to wear.

A locket shimmered as it fell to her hand,

Her heart felt new love appear so grand.

Now for life she'd make a new stand,

Helping others, a new life, a new land!

The child awoke with a sudden start!

Wild, oh wild, felt her heart!

Her mother was standing there by her side,

A question the child did then decide.

"Mother, I had a dream of a far away star,

Why do they twinkle away so far?"

Mother smiled "Stars twinkle as they sing their song,

This helps the world to be strong."

The child arose and walked to the mirror,

Happiness on her face did appear.

When she saw the locket sparkling so clear,

From the voice of "Barbara Star" so dear!

© 1986 Children's Rhyme Time Stories

Chapter Eleven – "The Bear and The Fish" by Third Oldest

There once was a very small fish,

Who had a very big wish.

He wanted a fish dish to kiss,

And this fish had to be a fine dish!

So fish went looking for his best gal,

To be his very finest looking pal.

But the only thing he found was a bear,

Bear didn't care, never did share,

And most fish didn't want bear to be there!

Now Mr. Bear met this lonely fish,

Bear thought hmmm, this looks like a fine dish!

But dish to fish meant how one looks and feels,

Dish to Mr. Bear meant how one tastes in a meal.

The both wanted a dish, but in two different days,

And one day, upon the water, the sun rays, did play.

Bear was there that day in water knee deep,

And fish (looking for his dish) did near bears paws did creep.

Now no one will ever hear a peep,

What happened that day when bear and fish did meet.

Chapter Twelve – "Spider in the Corner" by The Second Oldest

The spider in the corner was so forlorn,

He didn't have a stable home.

Seemed every day, his web ran astray,

He'd have to rebuild to get any prey.

Elderly lady kept dusting away,

Spotless cleaning everyday.

But at night those nasty cob webs came back,

Away, away, those webs she'd hack.

A compromise was soon made, you will see,

Elderly lady build an extra pantry.

So spider beside her, could now survive,

Stocking up on prey with pride!

Now elderly lady and spider live side by side,

Each respects the other's divide.

Peace and harmony they now do see,

They learned to respect each other's individuality.

© 1986 Children's Rhyme Time Stories

Chapter Thirteen – Teaching Without Preaching

Our children grow every day,

While listening to what we have to pray.

Our examples to them are on display,

We cannot just say, "Do as I say!"

Cause as we build our home's of heart,

Build with inner strength to start.

Live with love all about,

Then their spirits will joyfully shout!

Remember that life is like breathing,

You inhale of its wealth.

But you must also exhale and give,

This is in life, so we can all live.

Chapter Fourteen – Working Graveyard Shift

I started working graveyard shift,

Times to us, were all adrift.

Sending one child to school each day,

While other two kids with me at play.

Trying to stay awake, made me feel rummy,

I worked at night to keep us in money.

Husband would come home at night,

The house would look to be a fright!

Husband never helped me within the home,

That work was a woman's zone.

I am far from perfect, I know,

But once I had true love to show.

What I thought was a two way street,

Did unfortunately slowly delete.

I left and went to my sister's home,

She lived in the same neighborhood zone.

And gave me warm blanket and loving care,

I always want to stay with her there.

But I left and moved to another city,

Worked hard and tried to look half way pretty.

Chapter Fifteen – Looking For Work

I've been looking for a job diligently,

My budgets stretched my bellies empty.

No money to join a waitress union,

But I may participate in Holy Communion.

I don't need much to be extremely wealthy,

Just enough to be exceeding healthy.

Then I met a city man one day,

Never went back to husband in any way.

And married Tim, with his confident smile,

I traveled with him, many miles.

He seduced me with kind words and deeds,

I thought it met all of my needs.

I now look back on these years with tears,

Again abuse, gun shots, and many new fears.

He held a 38 one night to my head,

Alone I was sleeping within my bed.

And another night he came home acting so strange,

Talking nonsense and looking so vain.

I heard a crash in the bathroom that night,

I saw Tim, looking not right.

I hit his chest to get him breathing,

And once again I saw that he was living.

Soon I felt alone, nothing was giving,

I was his wife but life had no meaning.

I was so used to a life where there's no city strife,

I became "'Pinetreegirl living in the city life.'"

I am a Pinetree Girl, who just moved to the city world.

I am used to a life, where there's no city strife.

I'm Pinetree girl living in the city world.

Well we just moved there, to a brand new air,

But I do declare I'll be happy there.

Cause the arms that care, the arms we share, are also there, so I do declare, I'll be happy there, I'll be happy anywhere.

Cause he's a country man, making a city stand, in this city land, with his country hands.

I kept looking for work,

And found something that did not hurt.

Chapter Sixteen – Neighborhood Watch

I organized a neighborhood watch,

With Ernestino from our block.

Then set about and wrote this poem,

Hoping some other folks would join.

"Let's Mention, Crime Prevention"

Some time, long ago,

I could walk real slow, seeing faces all aglow.

I felt safe, love in the human race, keeping up with life's pace,

The world was not too hard to face.

Then I grew older, life seemed colder, crime appeared bolder, and

Children disappeared from one's shoulder.

So please let's mention, crime prevention, and start a convention,

A successful operation.

Together we might bring, security into being, and this security, can bring good prosperity.

Citizens can participate, making one's life accelerate, towards a safer and better date.Don't hesitate, don't wait, too late!

Help your neighbors, yourselves and your labors,

Please help prevent crime, cause I feel, and this is no line,

A city, without crime, can be divine.

Chapter Seventeen – School Closures/Busing Cuts

Then the city got rid of the school bus,

Many parents made a great fuss.

Getting to school would be a hard gait,

The lottery had just also been approved in this State.

So the tiny child headed off to school,

He'd be smart, seldom a fool.

But when he got to the street boulevard,

There was a street crossing guard.

Saying "go back home, getting to school's too hard,

Don't worry child, there's no detention card!"

Shaking his head, he dreamed of a bus,

Politely heading towards home he did silently cuss.

He wondered why education was no big fuss,

Oh well, he'd go home and play with Russ.

Our schools need our pride,

So education does not decline.

School closures so fast they decide,

Without listening to the parents outside.

Tiny child headed across the railroad tracks for home,

Knowing there he'd be alone.

Chapter Eighteen – Bad Times Again

Now times were getting hard again,

I hardly ever saw husband Tim.

Then one day he came home with Joan,

She started to arrange my home.

She was to be his new loving wife,

As for me, I was to start a new life.

He said our marriage had never been.

And the divorce papers I had never seen.

But he said we'd been married two days before,

My divorce was final from afore.

So Tim took our home, and all available,

If I filed for divorce, I'd end up in jail.

Bigamy would be forever my on my tail,

Always in life, said Tim, 'The *Male*.'

Then two days later while driving real slow,

The police pulled me over, no reason to show.

Asking if they could search my car,

Flashing me his silver star.

Under the seat, they found illegal speed,

That was all they did need.

To take me in to answer them,

I did not know where the problem did stem.

Tim provided bail that day,

I never was finger printed or booked in any way.

Was told just go to court some time tomorrow,

The attorney said to show the Judge some sorrow.

I didn't care, I'd done no wrong,

The attorney said "The charge would forever be gone."

Chapter Nineteen – To Shiver and Quiver

I woke up in new home with a song I did write,

Although the facts were not all right.

From where this song came it made me quiver,

I now had a song to deliver.

"The Big Fig Tree" Copyright 04-18-1986, Pau000825163.

Somebody shot a certain king in April of '68,

He was asking mankind please don't discriminate.

And now in January we can meditate,

Looking at what King was trying to contemplate.

He did a lot of good for lot of mankind you know,

Things I feel should have been done long ago.

But April 3rd somebody shot down that king,

And I wonder if the world ever learned anything.

Cause you say you're going to hang me from that big fig tree.

And I haven't done that much wrong.

You say you're going to hang me from that big fig tree,

And I swear I aint done that much wrong.

Now King heard Rosa Parks was dragged off the bus line,

Her feet could not move fast enough in time.

Now somebody wanted King to witness this,

Cause God's reasons all have a purpose.

As it was in the beginning, and always shall be,

What you give out in your lifetime comes back eventually,

In your eternity.

I gave this song to a church for free,

Leaving out the music respectfully.

My song was blues, in another key,

The pastor's music was religiously.

Next day I was driving around town,

Looking all around I found.

I was lost in that big, big city,

Everyone was black and handsomely pretty.

Being the only white person there,

For no reason known I felt a scare.

I pulled the car over by the curb,

People talking was all I heard.

But now my car, it would not start,

My heart turned like a wheel cart.

So I got out and started walking,

Came to two large doors I felt I was stalking.

A beautiful black woman answered my call,

When I rapped on these doors that were so tall.

She said "We've been waiting for you, it's true,

Pastor said you'd be here, he knew.

We've been waiting while we did pray,

Waiting for you this quiet day.

He said we know you by the clothes you wear,

They are soft like velvet I do swear."

Soon I came into a room full of people,

Realized I was in a church with a steeple.

Sat down and listened to the sermon.

Then got up and started murmuring.

I recited the sermon, but now in rhyme,

This was done for their specific time.

Then beautiful black woman got up in front of all,

Said "Do you realize, we'll have no fall?

This lady just repeated what the pastor preached,

It had same meaning and still did teach."

We all then sang beautiful songs,

A unified spirit, we all got along.

Joining hands as though we were one,

Feeling The Spirit, The Father, The Son.

Then turning to me she said "You may now go,

The car will start, I do know."

So I ran to my car, did not look back,

Scared of what they said was fact.

My car started away I did go,

Never looked back, never again did show.

That was me, it was meant for you to hear,

Although God's reasons are not very clear.

Chapter Twenty – Daleth

Years later I met Daleth,

He helped me fight off the rest.

Dealing with never ending insecurities,

And all my weird emotionalities.

Cause some people may judge you wrong,

Call you crazy and hurt you along.

What I call crazy is when lazy we,

Hurt another person intentionally.

Whether it be words or financially,

Especially is it is done physically.

So treat others the way you want to be treated,

Give them great big smiles when you are greeted.

For your life for another one was created,

And then love you'll see will be generated.

Sometimes I see Daleth running down the steep ravine.

I hear his echo of laughter, as though it were mine.

His voice causes the birds to stir,

They disperse into an unknown fur.

The smile on his lips belong only to him,

That smile, half grin, that lights up the eyes and my eyes.

I trip over a rock and pull myself up,

Running to meet and greet Daleth I stop.

Remembering that Daleth be not here,

He flew away with the angels one year.

The years have gone by now so fast,

My children helped me live to last.

The sad times are what made me strong,

Just remember this when things go wrong.

That yesterday makes you what you are today,

This so you can always stay.

Where you belong every day!

Chapter Twenty-One I-25 My Songs and Wyoming

Copyright 2-19-2008, Pau3-373-081

Going North on I-25,

My eyes did not feel quite alive.

I was swinging and swaying, not on the road was staying,

No more could I really drive.

An eighteen wheeler was going so slow,

Seemed to know where he would go.

It was then I did know,

His strength would bring me home!

Chorus:

Thank the Lord for truck drivers,

Cowboys and Sunday riders!

Thank the Lord for bringing me,

Safely home.

Thank the Lord for cowgirl ladies,

Rodeos and biscuits and gravy.

Thank the Lord for bringing me, safely home!

Now I knew there was a good man for me,

I met him eventually.

Never treated me cruelly,

Now complete happiness for me!

"Wyoming" Copyright 2-1-2008 Pau 3-373-096

I was travelin cross country, when I stopped in wonder at the beautiful sight!

Snow capped mountains, and old time cabins, dare I believe my eyes!

Well its wyo, wyo Wyoming.

That's where I want to stay.

Wyo, wyo, Wyoming,

I believe the Lord showed me the way!

Buffalo roaming and coyotes moaning,

A sight to behold!

Wyoming winds and trees that bend,

Feeling comfortably cold.

Well it wyo, wyo Wyoming.

That's where I want to stay!

Wyo, wyo, Wyoming,

I believe the Lord showed me the way!

Chapter Twenty-Two The Cowboy

The cowboy took off his hat,

Hanging it where it once had sat.

Cause home is where he comes to stay,

Living in his very lonely way.

Leaning back in his wooden rocker,

Picture of a gal in his hand.

He weeps for all he has lost,

In this prairie land.

That is where I found him,

Gentleness on his face.

Always a grin or a smile,

I knew I had found my place.

It seems he had all I had lost,

To get it back without a cost.

All was given back to me,

Materialistically and emotionally.

Seems I have traveled many miles,

But now I have many smiles.

All I have learned in my sorrow,

Made me what I am today and tomorrow.

Introduction

The wind was howling,

The man was prowling.

The woman was cowering,

Her courage was bowing.

Children crying in another room,

His silhouette upon her did loom.

He found her much too soon,

Locked within that tiny room.